The Flower Seeds

Acknowledgments
Executive Editor: Diane Sharpe
Supervising Editor: Stephanie Muller
Design Manager: Sharon Golden
Page Design: Ian Winton
Photography: Heather Angel: cover (top right), page 6; Chris Fairclough:
page 9; Image Bank: cover (bottom left), pages 23, 27; Alex Ramsay:
cover (bottom right), pages 13, 14, 18; Topham Picture Source: page 29.

ISBN 0-8114-3711-6

The
Flower
Seeds

Rosie Hankin

Illustrated by

Nick Ward

STECK-VAUGHN
COMPANY
ELEMENTARY · SECONDARY · ADULT · LIBRARY

Dad is going to plant seeds in the garden.

4

These seeds will grow into the biggest plants in the garden.

6

What kind of seeds are they?

Wait and see.

7

Digging lets more air into the soil.
This helps seeds grow.

9

Now the seeds can be planted.

I'm making little holes for the seeds.

10

The seeds will grow roots once
they are in the soil.

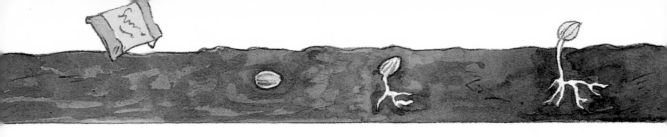

The seeds have sprouted. Now they are called seedlings.

13

The seedlings are growing quickly.

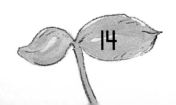

14

15

Your seedlings will grow to be taller than me someday.

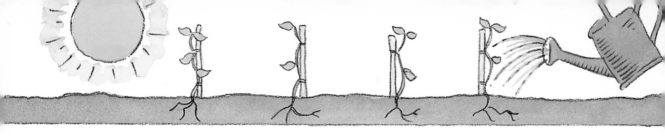

The young plants need support.

I'm tying the stems to these stakes.

18

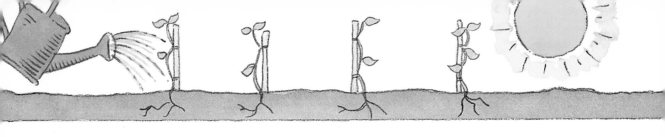

Plants get their food from the soil.
They also need sunlight and water.

19

Soon you will see what kind
of plants you grew.

The sunflowers have beautiful yellow petals. The flower heads are as big as plates.

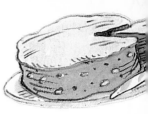

The sunflowers are only twenty weeks old, but they are very tall.

They are taller than Dad.

The bees are collecting a sweet liquid called nectar.

Now the sunflowers have lost all their petals. The flower heads have dried, too.

Look, they're full of seeds.

We'll plant these seeds next year.

Look at this picture of the growing stages of a sunflower. Can you point to the seeds, seedling, roots, stems, leaves, flower bud, flower heads and petals?

Index